AUGURY

Also by Eric Pankey

AUGURY

Poems

Eric Pankey

MILKWEED EDITIONS

Published 2017 by Milkweed Editions
Printed in the United States of America
Cover design by Mary Austin Speaker
Cover image by Johann Zahn, from *Oculus Artificialis Teledioptricus Sive Telescopium* (1685)
Author photo by Rachel Eliza Griffiths
17 18 19 20 21   5 4 3 2 1
First Edition

Milkweed Editions, an independent nonprofit publisher, gratefully acknowledges sus-
taining support from the Jerome Foundation; the Lindquist & Vennum Foundation; the
McKnight Foundation; the National Endowment for the Arts; the Target Foundation;
and other generous contributions from foundations, corporations, and individuals. Also,
this activity is made possible by the voters of Minnesota through a Minnesota State Arts
Board Operating Support grant, thanks to a legislative appropriation from the arts and
cultural heritage fund, and a grant from Wells Fargo. For a full listing of Milkweed
Editions supporters, please visit milkweed.org.

Library of Congress Cataloging-in-Publication Data

Names: Pankey, Eric, 1959- author.
Title: Augury : poems / Eric Pankey.
Description: First edition. | Minneapolis, Minnesota : Milkweed Editions,
2017. | Includes bibliographical references.
Identifiers: LCCN 2017007143 (print) | LCCN 2017014829 (ebook) | ISBN
9781571319401 (ebook) | ISBN 9781571314796 (softcover : acid-free paper)
Classification: LCC PS3566.A575 (ebook) | LCC PS3566.A575 A6 2017
(print) | DDC 811/.54--dc23
LC record available at https://lccn.loc.gov/2017007143

Milkweed Editions is committed to ecological stewardship. We strive to align our
book production practices with this principle, and to reduce the impact of our opera-
tions in the environment. We are a member of the Green Press Initiative, a nonprofit
coalition of publishers, manufacturers, and authors working to protect the world's
endangered forests and conserve natural resources.

For my granddaughter, Karlyn Ryan Steinberg

CONTENTS

AUGURY

AUGURY

Inside the camera obscura,
                    a cloud,
Or the image of a cloud, grows darker.
The past warps, curls back round to touch the present.

                    : :

Is it the spit and clay on the blind man's eyes
Or the little spell of words that returns sight?
Look, they said.
                    So I looked. But I saw nothing.

                    : :

A book of moths. A book of sand.
A book of stones unstitched from the wolf's belly.
Shot through with light,
                    a book of blank pages.

                    : :

The solution embodies yet keeps hidden
All dissolved within it,
                    keeps the hermetic
Hemmed in, the secret secret a bit longer.

                    : :

The Geiger counter's *tick-tick* like an old clock's.
Foreign voices on the shortwave, static
Like a mother's *shush*,
                    like crushed salt through a sieve.

: :

The past waits unmoved:
                              a rusted wrecking ball
In a vacant lot: a scoured erratic
Set down by a glacier—out of place, useless.

                    : :

A book of nuance that resists closure.
Book of Desire.
                    Book of the Vertigo of Desire.
Book in which the whole is latent in the partial.

                    : :

Rooks roost in the quarry cliffs; goldfinches
Flit and dart. Water long concealed in shadowed cisterns
Takes on a ferrous edge.
                    Look, they said.

2

SPECULATION ON SUFFERING

On a Babylonian bas-relief,
An antelope fawn's
Forelegs collapse;

Neck taut, it swings
Its head back
As a lion latches

Onto its hindquarters.
How stable a moment
Of suffering:

Fixed and fused to flesh,
The fold at the forward
Corner of the fawn's eye

Giving in, it looks like,
To sleep, yet the eye
Is wide open,

Attentive, not resigned,
But fraught, fearful,
Consumed by seeing.

ORACLE BONES

Beyond the word-house and sky-hung mountain,
Rain-frayed light burnishes the dusk-edged hour.
One can read the tossed owl bones as *empty-handed*,
Meaning *not yet* or *try again*, can cast forth into a future,
A dust-narrative of loose snow.
                                    Each is the same burden:
Not yet and *try again*—the lintel flame-licked,
Sleep banked in cold ash, a room furnished with smoke.
Each word on the page burned illegible.
But no matter, you know the story by heart.

SPECULATION ON A STAR-NURSERY

An empty, oarless
Boat drifts
Above vast depths,

Above silt
Stirred up like dust
In a star-nursery,

Where gravity
Long ago
Released light,

Light which has not
Reached an eye
That might behold it.

What is it
One sees in the place
Where the light

Will be,
But is not,
But is not yet?

EPIPHENOMENON

The lizard,
        born it seems of fissures,

Skims and quivers up the rock-wall,

Insinuates itself between chipped mortar
And a holdfast of lemon thyme

And is gone, resorbed again into stone.

                   : :

Another nameless spectacle,
                 the man thinks,

As he opens the door and a new day enters with him.

He moves from room to room,
Pulls the black crepe from the mirrors,

Finds himself reflected there in each.

SPECULATION ON THE HISTORY OF DRAWING

The tool,
A burnt stick,
Extends the body

In this space
And through time.
The mark renders,

We assume,
Asserts meaning
We might yet read:

An abstracted serpent,
The moon's trajectory,
A caribou's spine.

As far
As an arm can reach:
A drag of charcoal

High on the cave wall,
Still measured by,
Scaled to, a human body.

ELEGY FOR CY TWOMBLY

The water runs on—

A cold cursive stream—

An arcane meandering script—

An erasure of glare, once shadow-smudged, now
    rain-stippled—

Rivulets and tributaries—

Cramped, contorted marginalia—

Baroque pageantries of scribbles—

Calligraphic gestures kept in a daybook as light dims, limns
    into night—

THE FIG

Inside the fig there is a serpent
Beguiled by a beguiling serpent.

There is a breached levee, falling
And fallen stars, a grappling hook,

Icebergs in mist, megaliths,
A cache of Indian head nickels,

The invisible caught in the act
Of adhering to light, a matchbook

That warns *close cover before striking* . . .
But how to open the fig?

How to tear it asunder and,
In doing so, not mistake the plunder

For a petal-enfolded heart,
For a much-kissed mouth?

LOST

In the distance, a river
Like a faded line in an atlas,
But darker, given recent rain.

I know next to nothing,
Get by on nods and gestures,
Name things with the words I brought.

I turn back and take a new path
From some earlier point on the route.
The road bends to the left:

Dew at a web's interstices.
A stand of borage. Poppies.
The decline steepens, washes out.

In their feints and retreats,
Dragonflies throw off glints.
From here I can see the fortified wall.

DROPPED STITCHES

I learned first
             not to touch fire.
Only then to court it.

                    : :

The fig's autumnal black,
                              split open,
Reveals a raw red glare.

                    : :

I squint my eyes
             and the light spikes
Like rain frozen on a horse's mane.

                    : :

Between the green
             and the ripening,
An epoch passes.

                    : :

Like viper venom—
                    No—
Like tragedy fed on wolf's milk.

GHOST SHIP *or* UNION OF THE TORUS AND THE SPHERE

To reiterate the divine mysteries,
                                        mold
Wax and spices into the figure of an infant,
Call it *the offspring of an intrigue.*

: :

Dust attracts dust.
                        A cocoon of spun gold
Holds the slow barge of the moon,
The cold of snow-buffered echoes.

: :

At either end of the ship's long deck,
                                        two player pianos
Begin the same tune at the same moment:
The distance enough to muddle the melody.

: :

As if silence might be terminated
                                        by a cadence,
Or a closed lily remain stainless,
A cast spell calls forth favorable winds.

: :

How to leverage the ballast
                                weight of a grudge?
How to counterbalance one's own wretchedness?
The very act of weaving delays Ulysses's return.

12

: :

As the distance to the axis
                    of revolution decreases,
The ring torus becomes a horn torus, then a spindle torus,
And finally degenerates into a sphere.

: :

This morning they teach
                    the dead man's float.
Only yesterday did the children learn
To take in a deep breath and hold it.

: :

Venice, a silhouette,
                    hovers on evening mists—
Rough canvas tarpaulins, grayed, mildewed—
The decay and restoration cloaked.

: :

Acedia, it's said,
                    tampers with time,
Tears the soul asunder as a dog does a fawn.
Once ripped there is no mend, no repair.

AT SÉNANQUE ABBEY

Carbon pulls down lightning.
The charred tree, struck and re-struck
Over the years, sets buds, thrives

Nonetheless, above the forked,
Hollowed, and jagged ruin
Of its thrice-split, blackened trunk.

In its leaves light is written.

SPECULATION ON THE DARK AGES

Beneath a lexicon
Of fires, floods,
And invasions,

Deep within
A grammar of cinders,
Inundations,

And colluvium,
One finds amid
The toppled ramparts

And watchtowers,
An articulation of
A world that was,

However provisional,
Like the gas
And dust trail

Of an imploded,
Now vanished galaxy,
Illuminated.

SYNOPSIS OF A BATTLE

How steep the curve of forgetting.
How cold the fire that flint holds.
Bladder wrack in a backwash of waves

Catches on a severed arm.
Moonlight scours and scathes
The scrabble of uninterred dead.

Night like black shale
Weighs down the wounded,
Who call out or are dumbstruck.

Stuck in low tide marl, a thousand arrows—
Like reeds in the wind—
Lean back toward their archers.

SPECULATION ON MELANCHOLIA

The vanishing point
Is not a *point* exactly,
Shimmering, wobbling,

As it does, like a star.
I said, "I saw nothing,"
Not that there was nothing to see.

I turned toward Saturn,
The cold, airless
Shadow of Saturn.

To say the past is *fathomless*
Is to exaggerate;
To say the present *is* is not.

Distracted, attached
To an absence,
Attentive to only distractedness,

I mourned without loss,
Each grief reiterated,
Dulled by wear, yet undiminished.

PROOFS AND REFUTATIONS

A boat in the distance rows further into the distance,
Then more distant yet.

: :

A ghost moves on from those who remain—such noise and stink—
And fills in the voids of the past.

: :

A bit groggy, he deplaned and followed the crowd to customs,
Got in the passport line marked *Rest of the World.*

: :

What is lost when a language is lost, or rather when its last speaker
Has at last entered silence?

: :

Unhampered, a ghost moves on from those who remain,
Steps into a boat, rows more distant yet.

THE FRAGILE INSTANT THE NIGHT LIGHTS UP

The cloaked chameleon—element of *air*
In allegories of the four elements—
Embodied the gray gradients of the slate tile it traversed.

Although it was not transparent, I had seen through
The chameleon until it moved, until my eyes acted upon it,
And what, concealed, revealed itself as dart and slither.

READING MONTALE IN PROVENCE

I wait out noon in shade, back against
What remains of a retaining wall,
Watch a couple of men, off a ways, argue.

Guess at the implications of their gestures.
In the ditch bank, moon-white snails
Bend the blades and stems.

Beneath: hundreds of empty shells,
The bleached straw remains of last year's grasses.
The sun, irrecusable, is candid, not clear.

Ahead, road signs glare, scarcely legible.
To make such a light audible,
Cicadas abrade the heat with song.

SPECULATION ON THE LITTLE ICE AGE

A makeshift
Bird trap
Waits to be sprung.

A startled horse slips,
Sinks through ice.
Two women

With knives
Dress a pig carcass
Hung on a hook.

If you look up,
Smoke exits
Through doors and windows,

Because a stork
Nests on the chimney.
Twilight shadows lengthen,

Bleed into darkness.
Everywhere ice
Calls down the cold.

DOUBLE EXPOSURE

In the upland valleys: pasturelands and sheepfolds,
A clouded moon, plum-tinted with a yellowish blemish.

The obscure moon, Stevens writes, *lighting an obscure world*
Of things that would never be quite expressed . . .

The sky is dark porphyry and, below,
The sound of an unseen spring.

Rills and rivulets over loose rocks and fallen timber.
From that sound you recall the cool dank gloom of the
    Pantheon,

The transit of the oculus's light—its orb elongated,
Brightest where thickest—across the dome's curve.

The sound of an unseen spring and above
The sky is coffered and dark.

LOOSE LEAVES OF UNPURSUED SPECULATIONS

Discursive notations and diagrams,
Facsimiles and transcriptions;

Theories on the flight of birds,
The motion of waves, perspective
And optics;

       pages embossed
With rosemary leaves, a beetle's
Wing-husks, a star anise;

A single page blotted with ink;

On another, a smudged drawing
In charcoal: an overturned dory
Propped up with a stick as a rain shelter;

Watercolor copies of the landscape
Backgrounds in Leonardo's paintings;

A blank page rubbed to an ivory-like surface;

Many notes beginning *how*:

How to scry over water's still surface;

How to rid ravens from ruins;

How to make a firebrand with pine and birch bark;

How the exhalation of an angel is cold;

SPECULATION ON THE PRESENT TENSE

A gray stray light
Dims this moment
And the next

As if somehow
In the past tense:
Memory

That is, upon reflection,
Presentiment.
Ice floes nudge

And refreeze,
Break apart
And pile up.

What is fixed
Is fleeting
And what flees

Is insoluble:
A reconnaissance
Without end.

THIS IS THE HOUR

When the aftermath of sublimation and transmutation,
That alchemical slag called *darkness*,
Fills in the creases and crevices, the ruts and shallows—
When one, having lived too long
In exile inside a book, looks up and beholds,
As if an afterimage of the open book,
Blackened twin windows—

TWO STUDIES FOR A PARABLE

The mutable moon—irresolute, inconstant—
Is full: a source text of vacancy, a smudged page,
A poison ether that shimmers into matter.

Beneath it, the devil sows tares to choke the grain.

: :

The moon, a scrupulous eye, watches—bystander?
Accomplice? Who would believe its testimony:
Words chalk-dry, astringent, sluggishly plagiarized?

Surveilled, the devil sows tares beneath a full moon.

SPECULATION ON IMMANENCE

The room is
Unnoteworthy
Except for the dreams

Dreamt therein.
Its stone floor
Holds the night's

Damp cool.
Lusterless
Dawn shadows

Cover the room's length.
You recall
A cell such as this,

But it is dark:
A candle snuffed
And Magdalene's face

Still illuminated
By the skull
She consults.

REMOTE SENSING

Two rivers converge:
An austere fugue of grays,
Jade pendants carved in the shape of twin dragons.

Classical in proportion, order, and structure,
The day, seemingly motionless,
Is as liquid as the downward flow

Over centuries of a vessel's fired glaze.
The water's surface confirms
Opacity at noon. At dusk, depth.

The stars reflected there
At last at rest: so much dust in equilibrium.

SPECULATION ON THE WEIGHT OF YESTERDAY

Like a fish trap woven from grasses,
It allows passage of the element
In which it is suspended.

Like the light at Lascaux,
It is transparent
And dissolves as salt does on the tongue.

A fragile filament of graphite
Or three columbine seeds
Or a dime would tip the scales.

Rolled between your fingers,
It crumbles like a dried sage leaf
To fragrant dust wind disperses.

You wonder how such a small thing,
Removed as if a mote from your eye,
Could have caused such irritation.

Held in your palm, it is a smidgen,
An iota, a whit, nothing
A tear could not wash away.

NOON OUTSIDE THE CITY WALL

Now and then, cicadas cease,
Or the rooster in the valley starts up,
As if to remind the listener

Time passes. Beyond the gate,
If a footpath once cut through,
It is healed over now.

You can excavate the scents
But still not find the source:
Sweetness like a trellis of jasmine?

Or a melon cut open,
Tempered by a bitter note:
Ozone after lightning?

How many worked arrowheads
And spear points wait among
The gravel and boulders of a rockfall?

If only you could bend down
And snatch one up,
Feel where stone chipped stone,

Where, at the far end
Of the bevel,
A flaked edge still cuts.

ARS POETICA

The first people watch the drama of their fireside shadows and, even before the camp-following wolves lose their voices, the ritual sharing and eating of food replaces sacrifice

A forethought
A scrutiny before words

How easily words un–name
Slip like skin from a blanched peach

A yoke, a hand-carved wooden device, joined together a pair of draft animals, especially oxen. It consisted of a crosspiece with two bow-shaped pieces, each enclosing the head of an animal. The yoke is a tool to harness and focus energy, to allow the two draft animals to work efficiently together toward a singular end, often plowing or hauling heavy loads. Jesus, the son of a carpenter, who said *For my yoke is easy, and my burden is light*, would have known that the more perfectly fitted the yoke was to the particular oxen the more easily the animals could take advantage of the tool rather than struggle against it. The purpose of a well-made tool is that it eases and lightens work

Sand is heated to glass and lenses are ground,
Thus distance is bridged, or the otherwise invisible
magnified

It goes, we say, *without saying.* Nonetheless we say it

SPECULATION ON THE ABSENT GOD

As if abandoned
To plague,
The church

Under restoration
Is as of yet unrestored:
Awl marks

Score the plaster,
Spray paint tags
Mar the stone façade,

The scaffolding's
Aluminum pipes
And planks—

Rickety, vacated—
Are off-square, at a slant.
Kids play kick-the-can

With a dented censer.
With each kick:
A perfume of cinders.

THE LITTLE VILLAGE

Dusk as silent as an owl's wing.

The old wall, built by the Romans,
Or built to keep the Romans out,

Stands scaffolded and tarped for a long restoration.
Two roads wind around

To the mountain's top, where the little village
Hunches, half-concealed by shadow

Like the klieg-lit façade of an old movie set.
In the town square: a table set for a séance.

A stray dog turns around three times
Before settling down on the cobbles.

One of the six empty chairs at the table
Is toppled, as if someone

Had taken fright and stood suddenly.
The Ouija board's planchette

Hovers over *NO*.

CREATION MYTH

To render—to hold and preserve—is one motive.

Another is *the leaving of a mark.*
For a spine, a ruddy, curved length of line:

Ferrous oxide mixed with horse grease.
For the mare's distinguishing marks:

A palmful of crushed charcoal blown.
This is not the beginning of art,

But the beginning of history,
That is, a reading of what remains.

Art predates history, the lost outweighing

The preserved, and, thus, the at-hand
Is precious, embalmed

With significance, with signifying.
Gatherers, we gather the remnants:

Shards, flint tools, a granary door
Of breakaxe wood carved with serpents,

Or a cloth doll stuffed with straw,
And invent stories to fill in the space

Where not even the vestiges of stories remain.

INTELLIGENCE

Before creation
        darkness
Resides in a vessel called *the void*

No words to circumscribe the emptiness

        The background roughed-in, the foreground left blank

Blind spot: snow blind: the grainy, gritty surveillance footage:

At the curb, a discarded mattress, its intimate map of stains for
all to see

What looks like a body in the flames turns out to be a carved
    wooden guardian figure: millet-pasted, wrapped in jute,
    roofing nails driven into its skull

                    The regime photographs
      each of its victims. Marks in a ledger the years of de-
      tention, the means of torture, the date of execution
      or cause of death. The paper files are then digitized
      ". . . for ease of access, and if needed, discarding."

        Where the protesters
                set fire to a pyramid of tires
          a single flat rock tipped upright as an altar
              and dashed with blood
      once appeased the god

To excavate is to discover in retrospect—newness revealed by a lack of evidence in the subsequent lower levels

AT THE END OF THE LAST GLACIAL PERIOD

A herd flees,
                  fords the river's sun-bright passage—
A white incised line follows a bone burin—

To accentuate the counterpoint,
                          a sudden turn—
A gesture preserved, alive in the act of making a mark—

HIGH PASTURE

Horses gather, graze in high pasture.

On the rain-rich side of the range,
Rain.
      Here, cloud-broken sun.

At a loss for words, I write poems.

The rocks hold heat into evening.

BURNT OFFERING

Looked at long enough, an object
Deteriorates into discourse,
Which is to say: *which is to say.*

Amid diagrams, schema,
And theoretical paradigms,
You are asked to pick a number

Between zero and one.
Within that small gap: *infinity.*
But rather than the sublime's chill,

All you can feel is that the *felt*
Has been foreclosed upon, crossed out,
A useless asset from the start.

Abel's gift is not more worthy.
God accepts it to get things started,
To change a variable

And see where the tale might tumble.
Who is not tired of the wait
Through postponements and deferrals,

Through an infinity that just might be
Infinitely longer than the next,
Or the previous, which has yet to end?

VESPERS

Amid the fleeting subjects of light and weather
The invisible endures.

Three voices give rise to an absent fourth—

A low thrum of echoes—

Give body to all that the unseen
Underpins.

        A door opens to the west.
A shadow-procession shape-shifts to deep sky.

A note not there.
                The drone upon which harmony hangs.

SPECULATION ON THE VOLCANO

Moss on the outcrop.
Neither water nor stone,
But a sharp, grainy,

Mineral-tinged mist
At the foot of the falls.
Already yesterday

Is as weightless
As a sleepwalker,
As a ghost cloaked

Only in its name,
As smoke-architecture
A breeze tumbles.

Tonight, led astray
As always
By ancient starlight,

I'll let go
Of the ascetic desire
To subtract.

PINHOLE PHOTOGRAPH

The rivers, the Gasconade and the Missouri,
Converge, heavy with runoff,
                              and, although it's springtime,
Carry crisp, autumnal, balsamic, golden tones
Like some overgrown path to the region of the dead.

By shadow, I mean something luminescent:

First light leaking through closed shutters,
The oblong orbit of Pluto,
                              or the cave wall
The bison cross—an uneven, craggy landscape;
I mean what is gleaned from the silence,

Days kindled and quenched in measure.

ANOTHER TIME

She placed the flowers on the table
And felt the flaw on the vase's neck:
A crack as fine as fishbone in the glaze.
Even then she foresaw the crazes,
The fissures and chips, the ruined piece.

For her mother's wake, she walked the road,
Gathered bachelor's buttons, Queen Anne's lace,
And whatever else grew in the ditch.
The past, she'd learned, is like a fishhook—
Curved and barbed. It pierces and is set.

SPECULATION ON INVISIBILITY

Excluded from, denied entry,
One observes
And chronicles the long history

Of what remains:
Clusters of crockery on the table,
A dented copper saucepan,

And beyond, through a window
Uncurtained for such a view:
A mown field with crows,

A row of dense silver junipers.
Somewhere: a neglected detail.
The girl, for instance, at the door

With an ember in her hand,
Or Venus occulting the sun,
Or the sedated hive's writhe of smoke.

If one cannot see clearly,
Freud says, *one at least wants*
What is unclear to be in focus.

SPECULATION ON CAUSE AND EFFECT

The main character,
Born in a funeral home,
Lives at the raveled edge of an empire,

A paradise, of sorts,
She tends with ax-blows.
On the general store shelves:

A bolt of calico, a sack of flour,
Eleven kinds of penny candy.
She has ten pennies.

After the exhumation,
She climbs down in the hole
And watches the constellations turn.

The moon, fed nothing,
Is plump nonetheless,
Stomach distended.

One of the stars, out of line
(*That one*, she thinks. *No, that one*.)
Will set the story in motion.

THE CHANGELING

A sandbag levee held back the crest.
Each day was a minor tragedy averted.

Still miles away: lightning.
Or so the thunder said.

Wrought of hair, hemp, and sheep gut:
I was a changeling,

A ghost whose sole ambition was to be seen.
I nudged at embers to hear their hiss and lament.

Back then, shadow-lengths measured time.
Boredom, like mold, spread by spores.

Because he delivered milk,
The milkman wore white.

When, on the stoop, he set the bottles down,
They chimed brightly against their wire tote.

KANSAS CITY 1969

The boy is sent in to fetch his father.
The bar's dark is narrow and shallow,
Held down by cigarette smoke, a cloud

Backlit by a small black-and-white TV.
When the door shuts behind him,
The boy watches the smoke roil

And contort and he thinks of Judgment Day.
Little Jimmy, the barmaid calls him.
James is his father's name and not his.

Come to take your daddy home?
Shadows well between her breasts.
An unbuttoned blouse button

Holds on by a single raveled thread.
He thinks of the damned dangling
Above a pit of dull sulfur and magma.

Little Jimmy climbs a barstool and begins
To spin. He spins and spins, delirious.
He slips down off the stool and staggers.

STASIS IN MOTION *or* THE SHOWER SCENE IN DOUGLAS GORDON'S *24 HOUR PSYCHO* LASTS A HALF HOUR

You can watch on either side of the screen—permeable,
Stained like fine tracing paper with what shows through,

As if all you are ever shown is a copy of a copy of a copy.
Certainly, the door swollen with humidity would scrape its jamb,

And you would notice the masses of cool and warm air shift.
You would sense the presence of another altering the space.

Sometimes you can drive for miles and miles, lost in thought,
And recall nothing of the distance, the checked mirrors,

The lightning flash, or rain-darkened woods on either side.
It's a miracle you stayed in your lane as you hurtled—
        not mindlessly—

But rather sequestered in your mind, replaying the past,
The *what-ifs*, the ricochet of each choice, forgetting to adjust

For the weight of fate. Nonetheless, you haul a jack, lug wrench,
And spare in the trunk just in case. Yet the tire never blows.

You hold your hands up as the water falls around you,
And you feel as if it is miles and hours and not dirt you slough.

In the custody of gravity the water falls, finds the drain,
Sluices on. Your eyes closed but you keep on driving.

Best to find a place to spend the night, to get a fresh start from
        in the morning.
Best not to think of all the previous bodies the slack bed
        embraced.

ANEMOGRAPH

To represent the invisible,
A little dust swirls up and settles.

Or a shaken flame shimmers
Naked and without body.

Embers glow
On the blown-upon firebrand.

Wind in the sepulcher.
Wind to escort the soul.

Wind to lift up the saved
As all around the damned fall.

ST. LOUIS ELEGY

Only at evening's threshold—night's black gall as yet to fall—
Does he go down to the River des Peres:

The concrete channel dry, windswept,
A hint of snow on the air.

First he forgets which key goes in the lock,
Then which house is his. Then he claims he doesn't care.

Next to a trash can fire, he asks himself,
And God—where is God—detained somewhere?

The culvert dry, windswept. A hint of snow on the air.
Where else to find God but at the banks of the River Despair.

THE FRICTION BETWEEN A STRING AND BOW CALLS
FORTH A PLAINTIVE HYMN

At once emblem and instrument,

                the grain effigy sprouts from

    decay's ripe welter.

          : :

We train the vines to poles;

                steeped in time's ferment, we tread

    the grapes.

          : :

Floods carve a depth,

             animate an emptiness in which the

    river runs.

          : :

We abandon magic for faith, faith for science,

                    for which magic

    seems an apt substitute.

          : :

Look, on the horizon, the sun,

                a papyrus shallop, flares

    and sinks.

STUDY FOR *THE FALL OF THE REBEL ANGELS*

The rock ridge, worn sheer by millennia of mists,
Offers no foothold and, inaccessible,
Is believed to be the precinct of the sacred.

Before it, a hawk falls, then banks on rising air,
And crows, which harass the hawk,
Follow clumsily, less agile at such maneuvers.

SPECULATION ON THE AFTERLIFE

An herbal broom
Dragged across the floor
Cleans and perfumes

The chamber.
The ladder out,
Forged from lead,

Slumps beneath its own weight.
Mute in cold and darkness,
Sealed,

The chamber of the afterlife—
A vessel like a boat,
Dug out and buoyant—

Floats upon
All it displaces.
The hollow body,

Emptied of organs,
Stuffed with crumpled newspapers,
Along for the ride.

ANOTHER SPECULATION ON THE AFTERLIFE

Forgotten things
Disperse
As murmurless

As moths and rust.
Even the sense
Of *since*

Is now scumbled,
Indiscernible
From the chalk-dust

Of a thousand blackboards
Swept into a dune
The wind whittles down.

What will the soul
Do all day,
Unstitched from its body,

From the boredom
Of weather,
The weft of days?

SOUVENIR DE VOYAGE

What does one call a tree reduced by fire to a mineral? The quarry walls—tool-marked, wind-pitted—hold the last of first light on their scree-riddled edges. Stones excavated here were carved as columns, crowned with stylized acanthus leaves. Absent the whole, the part suffices. The edge of the Luberon is the same color as the tongue of a prairie rattler: a blue flash at bright noon.

: :

An image emerges from, disappears into, light. From the ruined half arch of an aqueduct, one imagines the distance coursed, the water's silvery shimmer like a struck string. A sudden gust of wind bangs a shutter. A spider, almost translucent, crosses an olive leaf. Hypnos bears a bouquet of poppies through a city built upon the air of its own name. Light again makes of a room a dwelling.

: :

I possess, I admit, a limited repertoire of themes and motifs. A hot breeze through the vineyard. Vines heavy with fruit still weeks from ripeness. In the middle distance: haze upon which, in the background, a mountain floats. I look up and I am a sickly boy again: writing an edifying dictum one hundred times in chalk. A white-on-green cursive alphabet runs the length of the blackboard.

: :

As night lifts up out of the valley, one stone-girded terrace at a time, and the rows of the vineyard and limestone grit of the goat and sheep paths submerge into the shallow surface of dusk, one recalls the weight of touch it takes to make a mark on paper, the pencil sharp, precarious, prone to breaking. The first mark is the horizon. Should the next intersect or run parallel?

: :

Upon a prone monolith—what will soon be repurposed as a tomb cover—figures crowd the depthless black niche of Caravaggio's *Deposition*. One man, holding Jesus by the knees, looks outside the frame for consolation. Overcome, we say, by grief. The pain mounts, but that is not the worst. It burrows in. One *becomes* grief—a stone in its stoniness, a worked lithic edge.

: :

The stone wall stands more tumble and ruin than wall. If not for a stretch of flawless masonwork, around which everything has fallen, one might have thought this load of rocks dumped here raw material for a new wall. Hard to imagine lifting each stone, turning it over and over in one's hands, attempting to puzzle it into place, never mind the scrapes, the backache, the wall, at last, standing.

: :

Beyond where the iron tracks bisect, steam lifts off the horses' backs. A dragonfly with mica wings hovers somehow, then darts. Farther down in the valley, a little fog broods. Each version of this tale highlights a different impediment. If the cicadas ever let up, one might hear a grub as it burrows beneath the tarry pine bark, or a green lizard skitter across the limestone gravel.

: :

A ghost, like a flame, is the shape of its consumption. A ghost exudes cold and one feels the change in the air as the ghost comes and goes. What one senses is experienced as a glimpse, a glimpse that outlives its moment. In the same way, a redacted text can disclose by its very withholding. The realm of God is like leaven, which a woman took and hid in three measures of flour.

: :

Here a child plays a game at dusk: she drops a pebble into a stone trough, disturbs the line of silt settled there at the bottom. Magritte says, *What resists our understanding lends a radiance to what we think we see.* Before dropping another pebble the girl waits for the silt to resettle. In that time, an ordinary wall beyond her is transformed by light, but the change, one might say, is imperceptible.

: :

Woke to the sound of horse hooves on cobbles, but from the window saw nothing but the vertical plume of cypresses, a glitter of green among the olives' dry leaves, how beneath the clothes' damp weight the line slumps. Went downstairs to the parlor, where an old sofa and unused piano convalesce, and looked out from there: only a tacked-up torn poster for a circus that never arrived.

: :

To look up at the stars is to experience the past as present, ancient light cast for future eyes, and this is that future: starless, cloud-covered. In the dark kitchen: the cold shine of a dented kettle, nectarines fresh from the market, aglow, spectral. When a car climbs the hill, a riotous gesticulation of shadows play across the wall and ceiling. The power's out. If you pace your steps, lightning lights a way.

: :

Above the narrow-streeted village: ivories and grays of an over-cast sky. To seek, avoid seeking. The church bells ring, yet hours elongate, hours foreshorten. The world is assembled in ocher and charcoal on cave walls. So little time between the dew-bent fern and peat, peat and lignite, lignite and anthracite. To evoke enigma, place two objects next to one another and step away.

: :

The poem is not a referent for experience, but an experience. The poem is a scale model of an invented place, an aggregate image, suffused, as an empty room is, with the various selves that occupied it and never returned. Yet desire and memory remain there like dust exposed on light-sensitive paper. Come. Enter as an arson investigator might into the aftermath of a light-obliterated space.

: :

Between a day that's ended and the one beginning: a narrow passage outside time. Don't expect to find there votaries of a vestigial cult of Dionysus, twin falcons rending the flank of a gazelle, or a shroud of jade squares held together with copper wire. There you'll find what Humphry Davy calls the *intimate actions of bodies upon each other, by which their appearance is altered, their identity destroyed.*

: :

The cold, greenish umber of a storm piles up. You are surprised, as when your host reached out to join hands and offer thanks for the food you were about to eat, the food she had prepared. The cold, greenish umber of a storm piles up and, where the mountains should be, a crisscross of lightning. *I have not made a habit of gratitude*, you think. Then the thunder, more delayed than you might have imagined.

: :

The ladder snake, our household god, prefers the cool beneath the stone stoop. She need not lift her head to note who has entered, who has gone. Emitting negative luminosity, she enthralls the mantis, the rhinoceros beetle, and the vole. They offer themselves as sacrifice. As befits a god, she has removed herself, keeps her own counsel. She speaks, when she speaks, in sibilant parables.

: :

Evening star like a keyhole into a barely lit room. The garden sparrow surveys its dominion. Except for a quartered lemon on a blue plate, the outdoor table is cleared. Those gathered are strangers to one another. Each has a room that faces the garden. They tell stories remote and practiced enough to sound true. As dark comes on, their gestures grow animated.

: :

Remnants of iron give jade its greenish hue. The yellow bough apple casts lavender shade. You find, instead of a map on the table, sheaves of scribbled field notes: *Exit where you find habit still shadowed by the sacramental. Turn where wind fords the river.* You crank the winch and haul up a bucket slung with water. After the sloshing settles, you look into the water. Not even your face is reflected there.

: :

The crag on which it's perched gives the church a melancholy disposition. The ruin, long quarried for building stones, open as it is to the elements, might not even contain the sacred. *Why not*, you have asked yourself again and again, *just turn away from the formless infinite, from the god-inflected sublime?* It is as if you have stepped into a clearing when your eyes had adjusted at last to the forest dark.

: :

Last night in a dream, you opened the armoire and found it to be a weathered harp case, and the harp, strung with chicken-wire, swung on hinges like a make-shift screen door. Sometimes, the edge of things can only be seen when looked at obliquely. Beyond the open door: the sound of rain in the dry, overgrown cherry orchard. Last year's cherries remained: wizened, rusted, unplundered.

: :

In Velázquez's painting "St. John the Evangelist on the Island of Patmos," John holds in his right hand a white quill—all but a few barbs plucked from its shaft—as he prepares to write in the blank book slumped over his left forearm and right thigh. He looks off and up to the right at some commotion in the clouds. The realm of God is like a field of crows heard long before it is happened upon.

: :

A storm dusts up and passes quickly. Lightning, a consuming blankness, leaps from the ground to the clouds then down again. Acrid ozone. Little corposant flares here and there to graph what fire fathers forth: this botch the demiurge calls *creation*. You have prayed to evade the incessant hum of thought. You have prayed for the angels to be silent so the unnaming might begin.

: :

To be god-filled is to be enthusiastic. *When a dot begins to move and become a line*, Paul Klee writes, *this requires time.* Things are what they seem to be: blood on the butcher's apron, plaster marred with scrawls and scratches, distance the deep cloud-shadow veils and discloses. In the old tales, the pursued mortals transmute into heady flora, into the diffuse light of constellations.

: :

A displaced object becomes charged with enigma. Placed in a vitrine, a specimen jar, or an archive box, the ordinary thing, now displayed and separate, safe from dust, from theft, from the merciless light, seems precious, vulnerable, and unattainable. Add now other objects, displayed in some irrational arrangement or in serried ranks. The viewer will perceive an organizing principle.

: :

The landscape, framed by my fourth-floor window—fields, vineyards, orchards—gleans the last luster of light. From this distance: the ruled stillness of a garden, the stroke of an hour prolonged. If not for the repetitions and tallies, this inquiry, as unstable as dust, would not proceed further. Memory, like a net, is more negative space than positive. For all the bounty, what has slipped through?

: :

As soon as we become motionless, Bachelard says, *we are elsewhere; we are dreaming in a world that is immense.* I observed a vine as it let go of its wire. Each day the vine pushes further: spills across the furrow and onto the field's rough edge near the rocky, gravelly path I follow. A ripe cluster of green translucent grapes, dragged along. As in a dream. Now, without trespass, within reach.

Notes

"Ghost Ship *or* Union of the Torus and the Sphere" is after Richard Serra.

"Double Exposure" is after and for Mark Desiderio.

"St. Louis Elegy" is in memory of Donald Finkel.

Acknowledgments

I offer sincere thanks to the editors of the following periodicals, where many of these poems, often in earlier version, first found readers:

Apartment: "Augury"
Cincinnati Review: "At Sénanque Abbey," "Vespers"
Concīs: "At the End of the Last Glacial Period"
Crazyhorse: "Ghost Ship *or* Union of the Torus and the Sphere," "Two Studies for a Parable," "The Friction Between a String and Bow Calls Forth a Plaintive Hymn"
December: "Intelligence," "Speculation on Invisibility," "Speculation on Melancholia"
Denver Quarterly: "Speculation on a Star-Nursery," "Speculation on the Volcano"
DistrictLit: "Burnt Offering"
Field: "Speculation on Cause and Effect"
Gris-Gris: "The Changeling"
Kenyon Review: "Ars Poetica"
Kenyon Review (online): "Speculation on the History of Drawing," "Speculation on the Little Ice Age"
Mary: A Journal of New Writing: "Dropped Stitches"
Missouri Review (online): "The Little Village," "Speculation on Suffering"
New England Review: "Speculation on the Weight of Yesterday"
New Letters: "Lost"
New Madrid: "Elegy for Cy Twombly," "This Is the Hour," "Anemograph"
New World Writing: "Synopsis of a Battle," "Remote Sensing," "Another Time," "Kansas City 1969"
Plume: "Speculation on the Absent God"
Sequestrum: "The Fig," "Noon Outside the City Wall"
Sou'wester: "Creation Myth"
Typo: "High Pasture"

UCITY Review: "St. Louis Elegy"

Verse: "*Souvenir de Voyage*"

Web Conjunctions: "Speculation on the Afterlife," "Another
    Speculation on the Afterlife"

Yale Review: "Epiphenomenon"

I am most grateful to the Brown Foundation for a fellowship and
residency at the Dora Maar House, where some of these poems
were finished and many begun. Special thanks to Katherine
Howe and Gwen Strauss for their hospitality and friendship in
Provence and to Nancy Negley for her philanthropy.

My deepest thanks to my sustaining friends, Allison Funk and
Jennifer Atkinson, for attentive readings of the book manuscript
in its various stages.

Thanks to all the good people at Milkweed Editions who have
made this book possible.

Eric Pankey is the author of twelve books of poetry. His poetry, essays, and reviews have appeared widely in such journals as the *Iowa Review*, *New Yorker*, and *Kenyon Review*. He is a professor of English and the Heritage Chair in Writing at George Mason University. He currently resides in Fairfax, Virginia.

Founded as a nonprofit organization in 1980, Milkweed Editions is an independent publisher. Our mission is to identify, nurture and publish transformative literature, and build an engaged community around it.

milkweed.org

Interior design by Mary Austin Speaker
Typeset in Bembo

Bembo was created in the 1920s under the direction of
printing historian Stanley Morison for the Monotype
Corporation. Bembo is based upon the 1495 design cut by
Francesco Griffo for Aldus Manutius, and named after the
first book to use the typeface, a small book by the poet
and cleric Pietro Bembo.

CPSIA information can be obtained
at www.ICGtesting.com
Printed in the USA
LVOW12s0146031017
550942LV00001B/1/P